Original title:
Harmony of the Hickory

Copyright © 2025 Creative Arts Management OÜ
All rights reserved.

Author: Christian Leclair
ISBN HARDBACK: 978-1-80567-346-0
ISBN PAPERBACK: 978-1-80567-645-4

Resting in Nature's Embrace

Underneath a leafy crown,
Squirrels toss their acorn frown.
Birds are in a silly dance,
Critters join with a wild prance.

Sunlight beams, a golden feast,
A chipmunk's joke, a funny beast.
Nature laughs, a gentle tease,
In this space, we're all at ease.

Tree of Tranquility

Beneath the trunk, a picnic spread,
With ants that march on all the bread.
A raccoon juggles some shiny spoons,
While frogs croak silly little tunes.

A whisper in the rustling breeze,
Can you hear those chuckling trees?
They tell us stories, oh so sly,
About the squirrels who dream to fly.

Intertwined in Earth's Breath

In the meadow, laughter swirls,
With dandelions and twirling girls.
Bumblebees buzzing a jazzy tune,
Doing the dance beneath the moon.

Roots below, a tangled joke,
While mushrooms giggle, then they poke.
A playful breeze lifts hats in flight,
Nature's comedy, pure delight.

The Language of Leaves

Leaves are chatting in the shade,
A gossip line that won't soon fade.
Acorns plotting a little spree,
While the wind laughs, 'Come dance with me!'

The branches sway, a merry jig,
As beetles strut, all snug and big.
In every rustle, joy takes root,
A silly song from tree to shoot.

Muse of the Woodland Heart

Under the trees, a squirrel's dance,
Chasing shadows with a cheeky prance.
Leaves whisper secrets, giggles in the air,
Nature's jesters joke without a care.

A rabbit hops in polka-dot shoes,
Daring the fox to join in the blues.
With every bounce, a chuckle erupts,
As the wise old owl just laughs and interrupts.

In this leafy realm, fun takes the lead,
Where laughter sprouts like a flowering seed.
The brook joins in with a bubbling tune,
While the crickets keep time by the light of the moon.

So raise a toast from your mossy seat,
To this woodland circus that can't be beat.
With friends like these, the world's not so stark,
For joy grows wild in this whimsical park.

Collective Mosaic of Greenery

In the garden, a gnome strikes a pose,
Winking at daisies, wearing garden clothes.
Butterflies giggle, flitting about,
Casting spells of laughter with every route.

A hedgehog rolls, a spike-ball of cheer,
While ants hold a meeting, sipping root beer.
Pillows of clover promise sweet dreams,
As the sun sets low, casting golden beams.

Toadstools bounce with mischievous glee,
Sprinkling their magic on each little bee.
The flowers exchange their funniest tales,
As the wind hums softly on its playful trails.

So gather your friends, let the fun take flight,
In this lively patch beneath the moonlight.
Each giggle and grin threads a story so bright,
Creating a tapestry of joy, pure delight.

Nature's Gentle Assembly

The trees all grab their fancy hats,
Squirrels dance in tiny spats.
Leaves jiggle in a silly sway,
While rabbits hop and laugh away.

Bumblebees buzz a merry tune,
Whistling birds join in at noon.
Even the mushrooms wear a grin,
As laughter echoes deep within.

Festival of the Forest Floor

Underfoot, the leaves do romp,
Fungi bounce, and acorns stomp.
The ants create a marching line,
In search of crumbs and drops of wine.

A pickle worm twirls with glee,
While mossy carpets sing for free.
Each critter adds a silly flair,
To this wild, boisterous affair.

Together in the Woodland

The hedgehogs have a tea party,
While raccoons play it all quite hearty.
Badgers juggle cans with pride,
As foxes cheer, they won't be shy.

The owls roll their eyes on high,
Watching dance-offs 'neath the sky.
Each creature brings a laugh or two,
In their furry, feathery crew.

Weaving Dreams in the Canopy

In the treetops, giggles ring,
Monkeys swing and do their thing.
Leaves whisper silly tales at night,
While fireflies flicker, bringing light.

Bats chatter about their day,
While trees sway in a playful way.
The dreams we weave in playful times,
Are full of laughs and jingle chimes.

Echoes of the Forest Floor

In the woods where squirrels play,
Acorns drop and roll away,
A chipmunk tries to take a seat,
But lands right on a beetle's feet.

The mushrooms giggle, what a sight,
As rabbits hop in sheer delight,
A raccoon sneezes, oh what fun,
The dew drops sparkle in the sun.

Treetop Serenade

High above, the birds do sing,
While the wind dances on a wing,
A crow just cawed, it's quite a song,
And now the frog is singing along.

The leaves shake hands with the breeze,
While ants march by with perfect ease,
A spider winks from his fine web,
While a snail leaves trails, no need to ebb.

Rhythm of the Rustling Boughs

Swaying branches, oh so loud,
Bouncing bugs make up a crowd,
A squirrel's cartwheel steals the show,
While nearby, a snail takes it slow.

The branches creak, a funny sound,
As critters dash all around,
A bear trips over his own feet,
And lands upon a pile of sweet.

Uniting Voices of the Grove

In the grove, all voices cheer,
A clamor of laughs, oh so clear,
A hedgehog trips, but never frowns,
While frogs wear crowns and pretend to bounce.

A chorus of giggles fills the air,
As fireflies light up everywhere,
While trees play tag with shadows long,
Laughter mingles, a silly song.

The Spirit of Verdant Unity

In the forest glee, the trees all sway,
Birds sing tunes in a comical way.
Squirrels debate which nut's the best,
While turtles nap, getting all the rest.

Frogs wear crowns of colorful leaves,
Crickets crack jokes that no one believes.
Rabbits hop round in jester-like prance,
While foxes all join for a dancelike chance.

Layers of Life Interwoven

Mice in disguise treat each day like a game,
While owls recite poetry, earning much fame.
A deer in a tutu twirls with delight,
As raccoons steal snacks, oh what a sight!

Beneath the tall trees, laughter resounds,
With bees buzzing tunes and nudging the hounds.
Ants hold a picnic with crumbs all around,
Where even the shadows make merry sound.

Cacophony of Silent Strength

A porcupine juggles while looking so proud,
And bears tell tales that would hush any crowd.
The wind plays a tune, mischievous and sly,
While butterflies laugh as they flutter on by.

Caterpillars argue about who's the best,
The laughter of trees puts their judgments to rest.
In the stillness, there's joy, bright and profound,
In this odd little world, where fun knows no bounds.

Chorus of the Woodland Spirits

Hippos adorn crowns of dainty old ferns,
While the wily old raccoon patiently learns.
A symphony echoes, played by the breeze,
With giggles from shadows beneath ancient trees.

Woodpeckers drum beats on splintered bark drums,
And worms write sonnets, in countersunk sums.
The squirrels all cheer with confetti of nuts,
In this woodland ensemble with raucous old cuts.

Celestial Connections in the Canopy

In the trees where squirrels play,
Chatting all throughout the day.
Birds gossip in vibrant flight,
How can they argue? They're all right!

Leaves giggle in the gentle breeze,
Tickling branches, oh what a tease!
Clouds eavesdrop with a puffed-up chin,
As laughter rises from within.

The moon grins down with a wink,
Crickets chirp, and it's time to drink.
Starry nights make each joke clear,
The forest friends are filled with cheer.

Nature's comedy troupe is vast,
Twirling tales from the future and past.
Every rustle and every shout,
Here in the green, laughter rings out!

The Stillness of Branching Lives

A turtle tripped on a tiny stump,
The hedgehog giggled, oh what a chump!
Every critter can't help but stare,
Who knew they'd laugh at a slow-moving bear?

The owl hooted with woeful glee,
As he watched the mishaps on the tree.
"I swear I saw it coming!" he said,
As a wayward branch bumped his head.

With flowers dancing in bright array,
They tease the bees who buzz all day.
"Keep your jacket on, dear snail friend,
It's spring, but we know this chill won't end!"

Every creature shares a plan,
To make each mishap part of the fun.
In this stillness of leaves and skies,
They find the joy in each surprise!

Where Roots Embrace the Sky

Roots twist and turn beneath the ground,
While branches sway, both up and down.
A spider spun a web of dreams,
In a place where nothing's as it seems.

Ants march proudly, a funny parade,
Pushing acorns like they're trade.
"Faster!" shouts the ladybug crew,
But their tiny legs just won't do!

Fungi laugh as they spread their spores,
Whispering secrets behind closed doors.
Mushroom jokes float in the air,
Tickling the leaves without a care.

The whole forest chuckles, it's so bright,
As roots reach high and grasp the light.
In this playful patch, they truly fly,
Where naught but laughter can deny!

Nature's Inclusive Gathering

A picnic spread on the forest floor,
Where mushrooms attend, and leaves adore.
Squirrels sip from acorn cups,
While raccoons throw in dance-filled ups!

Everyone's welcome, even the shy,
They join for fun, oh my, oh my!
The wind whispers jokes to the crowd,
And laughter rises, happy and loud.

As the sun peeks through the trees,
A game of tag begins with ease.
The rabbits hop and the frogs leap,
In this gathering, joy runs deep!

At dusk, they gather 'round for tales,
Of adventures through the winds and gales.
Nature's friendship, a mighty cheer,
In this wild wood, all are dear!

The Fusion of Flora and Fauna

In the forest, flowers dance,
Squirrels in a silly prance.
Bees keep buzzing, full of glee,
Chasing shadows, wild and free.

Budded blooms wear petals bright,
While frogs croak jokes to the night.
Trees giggle as the wind does play,
Tickling branches come what may.

A butterfly wears polka dots,
As rabbits try to tie their knots.
The sunbeam winks upon the brook,
Creating smiles—we're not a rook!

All around, the critters cheer,
As laughter rings from ear to ear.
In this mix of life and jest,
Every creature's simply blessed.

Beneath the Boughs' Embrace

Underneath the leafy smile,
A raccoon with a goofy style,
Wearing acorns on its head,
Looks like it's just out of bed.

A sleepy owl blinks with glee,
As turtles dance a slow, shifty spree.
The branches sway to secret tunes,
While the sky spills out joyful junes.

Fireflies wink in playful flight,
Chasing shadows in the night.
The boughs together softly swing,
As crickets chirp and owls sing.

A bear juggles berries up high,
While nearby, chipmunks just sigh.
Beneath the leaves, pure fun unfolds,
Tales of laughter, forever told.

Whispers in the Wildwood

In the woods where giggles flow,
Mice debate on who should glow.
Bunnies hop with such delight,
While badgers plan to steal the night.

The tall trees gossip, roots entwined,
Sharing secrets they have mined.
With each rustle, laughter springs,
Notes of joy the woodland sings.

A porcupine with quills so bright,
Wears a crown that sparkles light.
Squirrels share their tasty finds,
While everyone else hums in kinds.

Thus, beneath the leafy crest,
Creatures gather, feeling blessed.
With whispers soft and dances spry,
The wildwood's alive—oh my, oh my!

Resonance of Ancient Roots

Deep below, where stories grow,
Roots embrace, while shadows flow.
Tangled laughter, worms in glee,
   Spin their tales for all to see.

Above, the branches twist and twine,
Birds tweet songs, keeping time.
A squirrel juggles nuts and dreams,
While sunlight spills in playful beams.

The ancient bark chuckles along,
With echoes of a silly song.
Nature's symphony, a joyful jest,
Where every heartbeat feels like a fest.

As night falls, the fireflies glow,
Curly paths of light they tow.
The roots beneath, they sway and sway,
As woodland critters dance and play.

The Rhythm of Leafy Assemblies

Under the boughs, the squirrels prance,
Chasing shadows in a leafy dance.
They chatter loud, a noisy crew,
While birds join in with a tweet or two.

Acorns rain like nature's cheer,
As froggy croaks seem to draw near.
A turtle's slow and steady crawl,
While rabbits hop—what fun for all!

Tranquil Treetops Beckon

The wind whispers tales of old,
As branches sway, their secrets told.
Bumblebees buzz, undeterred,
Peeking in where roots have stirred.

A snail shimmies, shedding slime,
While leaves conspire to bide their time.
Mice tiptoe through the grass so green,
As giggles spread through the leafy scene.

Interlude in the Leaves

A chipmunk flips with nuts galore,
As blushing roses catch the score.
Caterpillars munch on sweet treats,
While fireflies perform for the chirping beats.

Mushrooms pop like cheerful hats,
As frogs compare their jumps in spats.
The sun dips low, a golden ray,
Nature's stage for a wacky play.

Seekers Beneath the Treetops

Fuzzy fungi boast of their might,
While dancing shadows twirl with delight.
A picnic spread, oh what a sight,
With ants competing in a food fight!

Lizards lounge in the sunshine's gleam,
While ladybugs plot their next big dream.
With each rustle, a giggle erupts,
Nature's jesters, all fun and hiccups!

Tales of the Timeless Trees

In the forest, squirrels dance,
Dropping acorns like a chance.
The wise old owl hoots a tune,
While raccoons play under the moon.

A tree once wore a hat of leaves,
Told the sun, "I'm one who believes!"
The wind replied with a gentle twist,
"Nature's party? You can't resist!"

Beneath the bark, secrets stir,
Where beetles hum the latest slur.
A pinecone jokes, "I'm on a roll!"
While mossy floors host a comedy show.

So come along, join the cheer,
Nature's antics bring good cheer.
Among branches, laughter swells,
In this forest, all is well.

Threads of Earth's Embrace

In the glade, the critters meet,
Telling tales with lively beat.
A chipmunk cracks a nutty joke,
While a turtle sits and smokes.

The grasses giggle, tickled by breeze,
As worms perform in tight little squeeze.
A daisy winked, said, "What a crew!"
While ants marched in, forming a queue.

Beneath the soil, secrets creep,
Where laughter echoes, buried deep.
Each root connected, bonds so sweet,
In this circle, all feel complete.

So raise a toast to earthen strings,
To all the joy that nature brings.
With every twist and turning thread,
A tapestry where silliness spreads.

Beneath the Sylvan Sky

Underneath the branches wide,
A ladybug takes a slide.
Snails compete in a race so slow,
While frogs cheer from a lily, you know!

The crickets chirp a lively beat,
As fireflies flash, all quite neat.
A fox in shades tells a pun,
"Why did the chicken cross? For fun!"

In the shade, the shadows dance,
Every critter gets a chance.
The brook gurgles with a laugh,
While kids play on its wobbly path.

So let's rejoice in this green stage,
With every laugh, we turn the page.
In nature's joke book, we find our place,
A world where silly dreams embrace.

The Awakening of the Underbrush

The bushes rustle with delight,
As critters wake from sleepy night.
A hedgehog yawned, its quills all spiked,
"Let's have fun! I'm not too psyched!"

A rambunctious rabbit hops about,
Practicing how to twist and shout.
The shrubs all giggle, wiggle, shake,
As bramble bushes join the wake.

A fox's laugh twirls through the air,
"Did you see the hare's new hair?"
With petals prancing in the dawn,
Nature giggles, curtains drawn.

So cheer for all that stirs below,
Where even roots get in on the show.
In this wild, amusing theatre space,
Every leaf holds a playful face.

Unison of the Underbrush

In the thicket where critters play,
Squirrels hold dance-offs, hip hooray!
The raccoon juggles acorns galore,
While the owl squawks, "Hey, there's more!"

Caterpillars twirl in a grand parade,
Bugs join in, none are afraid.
Even the hedgehog's in on the fun,
Rolling 'round like he's won a bun.

Synchronized Sighs of the Foliage

Trees twist in laughter with rustling leaves,
Tickling the breeze, oh how it weaves!
Bushes shake hands, they share a jest,
As the flowers giggle, they're all impressed.

The vines start winking, all sly and spry,
Whispering secrets, oh my, oh my!
With each rustle, they share a grin,
Nature's own comedy show begins.

The Meeting of Moss and Moonlight

Moss wears pajamas, cozy and bright,
Beneath the moon's chuckle, a shimmering sight.
Frogs croak their tunes, hip hop and sway,
While shadows play tag, not wanting to stay.

The night's so playful, it tickles the air,
Stars wink above, without a care.
A snail joins the party, slow but grand,
With a shell like a disco, oh isn't it planned!

Cadence of the Crisp Air

Crisp air has rhythm, a cheeky surprise,
Dancing past noses, it tickles our eyes.
Leaves act like maracas, shaking with cheer,
As the sun winks down on the frolicsome sphere.

The squirrels are drummers, beating on trunks,
While the brook's lively chatter adds giggly flunks.
Nature's jam session, what a delight,
As everything joins in, from morn 'til night.

Woodland Wanderings in Unity

In a grove where mushrooms chat,
Squirrels dance in a tophat,
The bushes gossip, oh so sly,
While rabbits hop to the nearby pie.

The trees wear coats of vibrant green,
Sharing laughs that can be seen!
A raccoon offers his wise advice,
Where trouble's found, just roll the dice.

A chipmunk juggles acorns with flair,
While the deer stop and stare,
Foxes play tag, oh what a sight,
In this woodland, all feels right!

With every rustle, a giggle spreads,
A parade of critters, all misled!
Together they brighten the forest floor,
Creating laughter forevermore!

The Spirit of Intertwined Paths

A turtle struts with a jaunty gait,
While crows plot mischief, isn't it fate?
The beetles roll letters from friends afar,
As squirrels bring snacks—a nutty bazaar!

Pinecones drop like gifts from the trees,
Fairies giggle as they catch the breeze,
Butterflies flit with a wink and a wig,
While porcupines dance, doing their jig!

Mice hold a party beside the creek,
With cheese and bread, it's quite the feast!
The sun dips low, stars start to spark,
Time to party till the skies go dark!

Every trail whispers a tale of fun,
Where chaos and joy have just begun,
With each step, laughter bubbles and springs,
In these woods, every creature sings!

Serendipity in the Shade

In the shade where shadows play,
A hedgehog plays hopscotch all day,
Frogs ribbit tunes to a lively beat,
While ants parade in a line so neat.

A worm wears glasses, reading a tome,
A dapper owl calls this place home,
Twilight tickles the leaves on the ground,
As critters gather, joy's abound!

Grasshoppers claim they're the best at tricks,
While turtles respond with their slow-motion flicks,
Laughter erupts like a popping balloon,
As everyone joins in this quirky tune!

The night approaches, but spirits are high,
With friendships woven under the sky,
In this glen of glee and delight,
Every creature shines so perfectly bright!

Fragments of the Forest Symphony

Whispers of breeze conduct the trees,
While owls hoot in perfect keys,
Mice on the strings play a fine duet,
With snails as the drummers, you bet!

The rivers respond with a splash and a curtsy,
As frogs jump in for a jazzy flurry,
A bumblebee buzzes the melody sweet,
While fireflies light up the fun little beat!

Raccoons join in, they tap and they prance,
On stumps they spin in a goofy dance,
With each piece sung, the night takes flight,
In this concert, humor takes the spotlight!

So here in the woods, let laughter resound,
With nature's own orchestra all around,
Just listen close, you'll hear it play,
A chorus of joy on a bright sunny day!

Collective Breath of the Land

In the meadow, cows wear shades,
Chasing clouds on lazy parades.
Pigs in boots dance the two-step,
While chickens gossip, secrets kept.

An owl hoots jokes in the night,
As fireflies twinkle, pure delight.
Grasshoppers strum their tiny guitars,
Just another day under the stars.

The geese are quacking, planning a dream,
While frogs jump in a splashy scheme.
Bees buzz around in a funky groove,
Nature's rhythm makes us all move.

So let's join the laughter, take a ride,
With all of earth, let joy provide.
In this land where laughter swells,
We share a giggle, and all is well.

Stories Rooted in Stillness

A turtle tells tales, slow yet grand,
About a snail race, and who's truly planned.
The squirrels debate, nuts or no nuts,
While ants march on, in tiny chutzpah struts.

Under the oak, whispers abound,
Where humor dances with roots in the ground.
Frogs recite sonnets, slipping on leaves,
And crickets chuckle, oh how time weaves!

Raccoons in masks plot a midnight feast,
With shadows amusing, they laugh at least.
Stories unwind like vines, sprawling wide,
In this stillness, where joy can't hide.

So gather around for a tale or two,
As twilight unfolds in a splendid hue.
With laughter and fun, we'll share this space,
In every still moment, we find our place.

Color of the Cool Canopy

In the woods where colors collide,
Birds wear hats, full of pride.
Sunlight peeks with a cheeky grin,
As squirrels play tag, not one to pin.

Leaves sway like dancers, twisting about,
While mushrooms laugh, no room for doubt.
The brook babbles silly little rhymes,
As nature giggles, in joyful chimes.

A parrot spills secrets, decked in bright hues,
While insects tap dance in their best shoes.
The breeze tickles trees, giggles out loud,
Nature's colors wear laughter like a shroud.

So join in the frolic, under this sky,
With each tickle and whisper, let's all fly.
In the playful embrace of this vibrant place,
We'll splash in the colors, and joy will chase.

Lullabies of the Leafy Realm

The leaves hum softly, a gentle tune,
While owls play chess under the moon.
Bears take naps, snoring in phase,
As crickets serve snacks, in their own ways.

Soft whispers drift through the silky air,
While bunnies gossip without a care.
The wind tickles branches, a playful tease,
And sloths share stories, moving with ease.

Stars twinkle brightly, a cosmic laugh,
As raccoons share pies, cut right in half.
The moon winks down with a cheeky gleam,
In this leafy realm, where we all dream.

So let's cuddle close, beneath the night,
With lullabies weaving cozy delight.
In the soft echo, of this woodland song,
We find our laughter, where we belong.

The Gentle Orchestra of Overheads

Birds are tuning up to sing,
Squirrels join in, a merry fling.
Peeking through the leafy dome,
Nature's choir calls us home.

Raccoons beat their drums at night,
With owls hooting, quite a sight.
The breeze sways, a natural band,
In a concert by nature's hand.

Colors of the Canopy Chorus

Leaves dance in colors bright and bold,
A confetti shower, a sight to behold.
Sunbeams play tag through shades of green,
Nature's brush paints a vibrant scene.

Each hue laughs, tickles the eyes,
In this quirky world where joy never dies.
Butterflies flutter, they twirl with glee,
A chromatic ballet, wild and free.

Echoes of the Enchanted Grove

Whispers of the wind tell jokes to the trees,
They giggle back with rustling leaves.
Mushrooms sprout with a cheeky grin,
As laughter echoes beneath their skin.

A fox cracks puns, oh so sly,
While crickets chirp as they reply.
The whole wood chuckles, a playful jest,
In this spot, laughter is the best.

Layers of Laughter in the Leaf Fall

As leaves tumble down in a fizzy spree,
They land with a giggle, oh so carefree.
Each crunch underfoot, a chewy sound,
A symphony of chuckles all around.

Dancing in piles, a whimsical riot,
Children laugh loud, what a delightful diet!
With every toss, a joy-filled thrall,
In this playful autumn, we all have a ball.

The Pulse of the Pines

In the woods where squirrels tease,
Pines sway gently with the breeze.
They dance with giggles, bark and bounce,
While frogs sing tales of a fish called Ounce.

Raccoons wear masks like sneaky thieves,
Stealing snacks from autumn leaves.
The pines are shaking, having a blast,
Nature's laughter echoes, unsurpassed.

A wild bear joins the leafy throng,
Clumsily stomping to nature's song.
He trips on roots and stumbles in style,
With a grin so wide, how could we not smile?

So come, let's prance beneath the trees,
With critters chatting and buzzing bees.
In every rustle, there's joy and glee,
Nature's giggles, come join the spree!

Crossroads of Bark and Leaf

At the crossroads where the branches sway,
Woodpeckers play their drum all day.
Leaves start to gossip, branches confide,
As chipmunks crack jokes, they never hide.

Mice in the meadow wear hats so fine,
While squirrels debate which nuts are divine.
A wise old owl gives a wink and a shout,
'This woodland life is what it's about!'

Under the sun, shadows twist and twirl,
A dandelion tickles a passing girl.
In laughter, the petals begin to pirouette,
Dance with the breeze, it's a joy to forget.

With trees like friends in a laughter spree,
Nature's playground is wild and free.
So come join the fun, let your cares be brief,
At the crossroads of bark and joy, find relief!

Tides of Tranquil Timberland

In the tranquil woods, a river flows,
Where fish are comedians, putting on shows.
They leap and splash with merry delight,
Turning the quiet into pure starlight.

A mischievous fox in a jolly cap,
Tells tales to the birds, who cackle and clap.
The water glitters, a joyous sight,
Reflecting the joy of the day and night.

The turtles waltz on their rocky stage,
While frogs recite poems, full of sage.
Breezes carry their laughter along,
In this forest theater, nothing feels wrong.

So let's dip our toes in this playful stream,
Life's a grand joke; nature's the theme.
Where water and woods forever entwine,
Laughter lingers, making all things fine!

Refuge Beneath the Great Green

Beneath the great green, where laughter grows,
The trees share secrets that nobody knows.
A frisky raccoon twirls with glee,
As squirrels play tag, oh, what a spree!

Fluttering leaves in the cool, sweet air,
Whisper to bunnies who scamper without care.
A ladybug cracks jokes with no fear,
In the realm of the green, fun is near!

The wise old tree chuckles, its trunk so wide,
As the critters gather, giggling side by side.
They swap funny tales of their woodland feats,
In this enchanted grove, joy endlessly greets.

So let's all nestle in nature's embrace,
Where joy and laughter set the pace.
In this refuge, the world feels right,
Beneath the great green, there's pure delight!

Confluence at the Forest's Edge

In the woods where squirrels dance,
A rabbit tries to take a chance.
He leaps and bounds with all his might,
But lands on mushrooms—what a sight!

The owls hoot jokes from trees so tall,
While chipmunks gather snacks for all.
A deer shares tales of antics wild,
With laughter echoing, all beguiled.

Beneath the pines, the laughter flows,
As bees all buzz in rhyming prose.
The sun peeks in, joins the fun,
As nature's party's just begun!

With every rustle, giggles swell,
The forest whispers, "All is well!"
A confluence of joy fills the air,
In this woodland fest, without a care.

A Tapestry of Treetops

In the canopy, a parrot sings,
While monkey swings with silly flings.
The crows play cards with acorn bets,
And squirrels giggle at their debts.

A woodpecker drums a funny beat,
While beavers organize a treat.
A soup of leaves, a stew of bark,
They feast together till it's dark.

With branches low, a bench is made,
For all to share in this parade.
The raccoons nap, dreaming of snacks,
As owls plot pranks—what funny hacks!

Underneath the stars, they tease and poke,
With every quip, laughter awoke.
A tapestry of joy they weave,
In this charming home, one can believe.

Soulful Conversations Among the Roots

Beneath the trees, where shadows play,
A turtle tells his tales of sway.
Each story laced with humor wise,
While caterpillars roll their eyes.

The roots entwine in gossipy chats,
As wise old toads poke fun at bats.
With wiggles and giggles, they unfold,
A symphony of laughter, bold.

A gopher jokes about his digs,
As fireflies flash like tiny digs.
The ground feels warm, the mood is bright,
In this rooty realm, all feels right.

With every chuckle, bonds grow tight,
In the heart of nature, pure delight.
Soulful moments drench the ground,
A perfect world where joy is found.

The Interconnection of Life

A rabbit hops and sees a snail,
"Come join the race!" he starts to wail.
The snail replies, "I'll win in time!"
They giggle as they bound in rhyme.

The ants parade with tiny feet,
As crickets chirp a rhythmic beat.
A tree trunk hums with jokes so sly,
While owls maintain their watchful eye.

Every critter joins the fray,
With puns and jests that lead the way.
From roots to boughs, the fun extends,
As nature's pulse through laughter blends.

Together here, life intertwines,
In little quirks, the joy aligns.
In this grand show of vibrant jest,
Every being finds their place, so blessed.

Nature's Serenade at Dusk

The crickets chirp a wacky tune,
While fireflies dance beneath the moon.
Raccoons hold a midnight feast,
And squirrels plan a nutty beast.

The owls hoot with cheeky flair,
Wishing they could join the fair.
Cats yawn and stretch, a slow display,
Pretending not to care, but they play.

With every breeze, a giggle flows,
As leaves rustle in the throes.
A rabbit hops with joyful might,
And the world chuckles at the sight.

As night falls softly on the glade,
We laugh and sing, unafraid.
In nature's jest, we find delight,
In twilight's glow, all feels just right.

The Tranquil Interlude of Timber

In the forest, a calm prevails,
Yet mischief lurks in leafy trails.
A bear tries yoga, takes a spill,
While otters glide, showcasing skill.

The saplings whisper cheeky tales,
Of wise old trees and tiny snails.
A bunny dons a dapper hat,
And takes a stroll, just fancy that!

The woodpecker drums a silly beat,
While turtles take a lazy seat.
Each critter knows their role to play,
In this wild, whimsical ballet.

Time meanders like a lazy creek,
Where laughter echoes, no need to sneak.
In quiet revelry, we unite,
Sharing giggles 'til the night.

Voices in the Verdant Vale

The brook babbles with a wink,
While mushrooms wear hats, don't you think?
Frogs croak jokes from the lily pads,
Making us laugh, oh! Aren't they rad?

A deer takes a step, trips on a stone,
Dancing, we laugh, but she's not alone.
A band of critters forms a crew,
Playing tunes on bamboo, just for you!

The grasshoppers leap with flair and zeal,
While chipmunks spin a crazy wheel.
In this vale, joy's the only plan,
Nature's jesters, oh what a clan!

As dusk settles, the laughter swells,
With echoes of fun, no need for bells.
In the verdant vale, we find our play,
Chasing the sun till the end of the day.

The Acorn's Gentle Refrain

An acorn winks from the great oak tree,
   Singing softly, 'Come and see!'
A gathering forms, all furry and bright,
   Chakra chips and nutty delight.

The chipmunks chatter, "What's the plan?"
   As gatherers munch beneath the span.
Squirrels flip over, twirling with glee,
   In a nutty dance, wild and free.

Birds chirp catchy little songs,
Joining in, where laughter belongs.
A turtle shuffles, slow and proud,
While the critters cheer, they form a crowd.

Under canopies, joy turns to feast,
In nature's realm, spirits released.
With each acorn drop, a jolly refrain,
Reminds us all, life's just a game.

Gathering Shadows at Dusk

As the sun dips low, the squirrels meet,
They trade their secrets and a nutty treat.
A raccoon joins in with a sly little grin,
Planning mischief while the night starts to thin.

Owls hoot softly, in feathery attire,
While crickets chirp tunes to fuel the fire.
The shadows stretch long, like a cat on a spree,
Casting laughter, as the dusk calls for glee.

Chipmunks create a game of hide and seek,
In the arms of the trees, they play hideously cheek.
But the fireflies wink, lighting paths with great flair,
Giving the night a mischievous glare.

So gather ye round, let's dance with delight,
Underneath starlit skies, through the whimsical night.
In the dark, we find fun, a sprinkle of glee,
Nature's own circus, wild and free!

Sunlit Reverie Among the Foliage

Beneath the trees where the sunbeams play,
A toad sings loud, come join in today!
The butterflies giggle, flitter and flap,
As the bumblebees buzz about with a snap!

Ferns wave hello to their leafy friends,
While the beetles roll by, not making amends.
With blossoms so bright, it's a party of cheer,
Even the ants march, and there's nothing to fear!

A jolly old fox dons his finest bow tie,
Twirling and prancing, oh my, oh my!
He entertains deer with a joke or a pun,
In the sunlit glade, everyone's having fun.

So come take a stroll, unwind with these sights,
Join the playful dance of the magical lights.
In the midst of the foliage, we all unite,
For laughter and joy make the day feel just right!

Bonds of the Wooded Realm

In the thicket where giggles blend with sighs,
A raccoon insists he's the king of the pies.
He juggles wild berries, such a comical sight,
While the rabbits all cheer him with sheer delight.

Squirrels throw acorns, like tiny grenades,
While the hedgehogs laugh in their spiky charades.
The tall trees lean in to hear each jest,
In this wooded domain where laughter's the best.

The gnomes all agree, it's a splendid old place,
Where mischief abounds at a leisurely pace.
A porcupine struts, and the chipmunks all sing,
Celebrating the bonds that nature can bring.

So gather ye close, in this realm of the green,
Where every leaf rustles holds secrets unseen.
With laughter as glue, we bind all our dreams,
In the woods, all is bright, or so it seems!

Unbroken Circles of Green

In the heart of the grove, where the laughter is loud,
Whispers of ferns form a giggling crowd.
The grasshoppers dance in a merry parade,
While the wise old owls watch, bemused and unafraid.

A frog croaks a tune on a sweet lilypad,
And a turtle joins in—oh, how it's mad!
With a flip and a flop, they create quite a scene,
In the circles unbroken, both vibrant and green.

The bees buzz their tunes, while the daisies tap feet,
Creating a rhythm that's oh-so-sweet.
Even the rocks chuckle in laughter's embrace,
As the sun blesses all with its warm, golden grace.

So frolic and play, in this joyful domain,
Where the trees hum a song, and the skies never feign.
In the unbroken circles, we find our own song,
In the symphony of laughter, we truly belong!

Rhythms of the Rooted Souls

Underneath the ground they dance,
With roots entwined, they take a chance.
Their silly moves cause quite a scene,
In the soil's ball, they're the routine.

The worms all cheer, the bugs won't stop,
As tangled twigs go hop, hop, hop.
Their leafy hats bob in delight,
Branching out to groove all night.

When breezes blow, they sway and spin,
Beneath the stars, they all begin.
"Twirl like a top!" the saplings shout,
The laughing buds can't live without.

With acorns clapping on the ground,
A funny beat that's world-renowned.
So join the fun, no need for grace,
Just wiggle, giggle, join the race!

Lullabies of the Leafy Giants

The giants murmur soft and low,
With rustling leaves, they start the show.
While owls snooze beneath the bark,
The branches hum tunes in the dark.

Squirrels yawn, then start to sway,
Chasing dreams while night turns day.
Their fluffy tails dance with ease,
Tickling the breeze among the trees.

With playful whispers, they convene,
As moonbeams paint their shades of green.
A lullaby of chuckles bright,
Rock-a-bye, dear leaves, goodnight, goodnight.

In dreams, they're riding on the wind,
Strumming chords that won't rescind.
The sleepy buds in gentle flight,
Snuggle close till morning light.

A Tapestry of Twigs and Time

Woven in the forest's seam,
Twigs dance wildly, living a dream.
With every knot and twist they make,
A funny story starts to wake.

They gossip with the passing breeze,
Sharing laughs with friendly trees.
"Did you hear the tale of that vine?
It tried to climb but lost its spine!"

By day they thread through sun and shade,
At night they glow as fireflies parade.
A tapestry of giggles bright,
Can make even the stars feel light.

So join the party, grab a twig,
Come tell a tale that's sure to dig.
Together we'll weave laughter and cheer,
In the fabric of life, let's give a cheer!

Chords of the Climbing Vines

Vines wiggle up the trees so spry,
With leafy fingers reaching high.
They play the music of the tall,
Each note a giggle, a leafy call.

As they stretch up to the sky,
"Let's start a band!" the flowers cry.
With petals clapping, a funny show,
The climbing vines begin to glow.

Swinging low and jiving fast,
Their musical notes are unsurpassed.
The dandelions hum along,
While lively ants tap to the song.

In unison, they dance and play,
A grassy fandango to greet the day.
Join in their cheer, give it a go,
With vines and buds in a joyful flow!

Bond Forged in Forest Depths

In the woods, where squirrels play,
They barter acorns, day by day.
A raccoon's laugh rings through the tree,
While owls roll eyes, as wise as can be.

The trees join in a goofy dance,
As critters prance in wild romance.
A chipmunk sneezes, all freeze in dread,
But laughter erupts, life's simple thread.

Bark-scratch duets, a majestic scene,
A beetle's waltz, like none you've seen.
In this glen of giggles and glee,
Adventures bloom, wild and free.

So here's to friends, both furry and feathery,
Creating joy, never a dull tread.
In the depths of the woods, we find our cheer,
With chuckling leaves, we hold so dear.

Serenity in the Shade

Underneath the leafy green,
A sleepy snail stirs, then's seen.
With dreams of racing on a whim,
But just a nap, it seems, suits him.

The dappled sun plays hide and seek,
While gophers giggle, taking a peek.
A wise old turtle sips his tea,
"Why rush?" he grins, "Just chill with me!"

Sunlight tickles the patchy ground,
As frogs compose a croaky sound.
Each playful note a sweet refrain,
In shaded spots, we dance in rain.

With chatter from a friendly crow,
Mirth wraps around, it's quite the show.
So let's kick back, in shadows laid,
Embracing all that shade has made.

Cradle of the Copse

In a nook where the wild things thrive,
A hedgehog dons a spiky jive.
With every roll, a giggle grows,
While butterflies share silly bows.

The whispers of grass tickle the toes,
As dancing daisies come and pose.
A game of tag with rabbits in flight,
Turns a morn into sheer delight.

Blue jays flaunt their royal crest,
While otters splash, just like the rest.
A chorus rings, a joyful note,
From every nook, the laughter floats.

Underneath the great oak's spread,
We build our dreams, onward we tread.
In this cradle, wild and bright,
We find our joy, pure and light.

Journey Through the Interwoven

Twisting trails through tangled vines,
We stumble on, as nature shines.
A fox trips over its own feet,
While all around, the woodland greets.

Rabbits hop with giggles shared,
A deer pauses, slightly scared.
But a raccoon waves, "Come, join the fun!"
With every quirk, a smile's begun.

In intertwining tales we spin,
As frogs make bets on who'll jump in.
The trees chuckle, make no fuss,
Just offer shade for all of us.

So we roam through this laughing maze,
In the lush embrace, we spin our days.
From tangled threads, a tapestry bright,
In laughter's weave, we find our light.

Whims of the Whispering Woods

In the woods where the squirrels dance,
The rabbits leap in a silly prance.
A fox with a hat grips its own grande cup,
Sipping tea, saying, "What's up?"

The trees chuckle, leaves in a whirl,
As the daisies gossip, petals unfurl.
A raccoon in glasses, reading the news,
Whispers secrets, spreading the blues.

The owls hoot jokes, wise as can be,
While the deer try to swallow their tea.
The brook sings tunes that tickle the toes,
In this cheerful place, laughter overflows.

Under the Shade of Togetherness

Beneath the branches, a picnic spree,
Ants gather snacks like a party, whee!
A bear in a bow tie breaks bread with a bee,
Sharing honey talk, delightful and free.

The mushrooms giggle, dressed in bright spots,
While the turtles play checkers, tied in their knots.
A badger complains, 'It's hot in the sun!'
"Just chill," says the hedgehog, "We're having fun!"

Chirps from the birds, the melody's loose,
The fish in the pond throw in their own juice.
As laughter echoes, a frog starts to croak,
They'll toast with some dew—nature's fine joke.

A Gathering of Woodland Whisperers

In a groove where the creatures convene,
A raccoon dons shades, oh what a scene!
The porcupine strums, sees a rock band rise,
While the fireflies blink like the stars in their eyes.

Bats plan a dance, twirling with flair,
Frogs join the fun, leaping through air.
"Let's throw a party!" a cheeky crow caws,
And the owls roll in, taking a pause.

Hiccups from hedgehogs, laughing in fright,
Squirrels share acorns, a comedic sight.
As moonlight spills, the night grows bright,
In this wood's circus, all feels just right.

Lost in the Embrace of Nature

A moose wears a scarf, looking quite grand,
Sipping on smoothies, drawing in sand.
The trees sway, gossiping low about fun,
While chipmunks take selfies—smile, everyone!

The clouds toss popcorn, rain drips like cheer,
The beetles join in, a conga line near.
"It's a wild world!" says a lizard on branch,
"Let's spin in the wind, go ahead, take a chance!"

A creek's laughter bubbles over the stones,
As frogs sit with popcorn, all making tones.
Lost in this laughter, joy swings and spins,
Nature's embrace leaves no room for sins.

Shadows of Togetherness

In the shade of the trees, they dance with glee,
Squirrels in suits, as fancy as can be.
A raccoon in a top hat, sipping on tea,
Laughing at whispers, just you and me.

Birds chirp the tune of a quirky parade,
While the fox plays the drums, never afraid.
The breeze cracks a joke, oh ain't that a delight,
Nature's own comedy that feels just right.

Laughter erupts from the bushes nearby,
While the deer try to figure out how to fly.
The plants are all giggling, quite out of control,
Tickled by tickles of a bellyful soul.

So come spread your arms, get lost in the swarm,
In this woodland circus, it's all quite the charm.
Under leafy balloons that dance above,
Let's toast to the silliness — nature's pure love.

The Quietude of the Swaying Grove

In a grove where the shadows play hide and seek,
Trees wear pajamas, they're far from bleak.
Breezes whisper secrets with giggly sighs,
As a curl of mist laughs and rolls through the skies.

Frogs croak in chorus, a comedic show,
While the owls wink their eyes, putting on quite a glow.
Leaves flutter and flutter, like giggling friends,
Sharing their tales where the laughter never ends.

A rabbit in slippers jumps over the brook,
While turtles with hats read their favorite book.
The crunch of the twigs underneath paws so light,
In this serene place, everything feels right.

Mushrooms wear crowns, moss is their gown,
Fluffy clouds above don't seem to frown.
So join in the fun, let your worries drift,
In this peaceful grove, smile is the gift.

Kinship of Nature's Palette

Colors collide in a splashy surprise,
Flowers paint murals, a feast for the eyes.
The daisies make jokes with the tulips so bright,
While bees bring the nectar, buzzing with might.

The sun winks down in a golden parade,
As butterflies giggle, in fairies' charade.
Each leaf has a story, a tale to unveil,
In this jesting garden where laughter prevails.

Clouds join in, soft, as they drape on the sky,
Telling ticklish stories as they wander by.
Breezes carry chuckles, a tickle of cheer,
In this colorful world, joy's ever near.

So let's skip on the petals, with hearts open wide,
In this merry landscape, let's take a fun ride.
Nature's a canvas, with smiles and delight,
Join hands with the daisies, oh what a sight!

Melodies in the Meadow

In the meadow where giggles grow wild and free,
Grasshoppers sing tunes under a shady tree.
Sunflowers sway to the rhythm of cheer,
While butterflies flit like they've got nothing to fear.

Bees buzz a beat, while frogs croon away,
Lively tunes echo at the end of the day.
Clouds float along, bobbing to the song,
In this cheerful place, you can't help but belong.

The daisies are dancers, twirling so bright,
All nature conspired for a musical night.
Breezes act as conductors, waving their hands,
As critters join in to form whimsical bands.

So come take a break, let your spirit take flight,
Join the fun here, everything feels just right.
In the meadow's embrace, with laughter and song,
Nature's own choreography, inviting you along.

Dance of Leaves in Twilight

In twilight's glow, they spin and swirl,
The leaves in laughter, a merry whirl.
Branches clap like hands, a joyful cheer,
As shadows play tag, with no hint of fear.

Squirrels wear hats, quite silly indeed,
While rabbits do jig, a grass-fueled creed.
Frogs on the pond jump in time, oh delight,
Each jump a giggle, a whimsical sight.

Embrace of the Elder Trees

Old trees with wrinkles, tell tales they know,
Their branches stretch out, putting on a show.
With roots intertwined, they share a big hug,
While insects all dance in a happy slug rug.

"Hang tight!" whispers one, as a breeze rolls by,
"Let's tickle the birds, watch them flutter and fly."
And squirrels drop acorns, their own little pranks,
As laughter erupts from the elder tree ranks.

Symphony of Serene Shores

The waves strum softly, a ticklish chorus,
Seagulls croon loudly, their antics wondrous.
Sand fiddles play, while crabs tap their feet,
A beach bash erupts, oh, isn't it sweet?

Starfish in shades strut with style, oh my!
Seashells hold dance-offs, who knows who'll fly?
Each splash is a note, and laughter a song,
Like a hidden treasure, where silliness belongs.

Melodies Beneath the Canopy

Beneath the green roof, where shadows create,
Critters join in, it's a concert, feel great!
The stalks bend in rhythm, they sway and they bend,
While beetles find instruments, a tune to send.

A cricket on drums, with a beat oh so neat,
And ants doing cha-cha, oh, what a feat!
In the heart of the grove, the laughter is clear,
Nature's own band, come join us, oh dear!

Whispers of the Woodland

In the woods where squirrels roam,
They plot their sneaky little combs.
With acorns stacked in tiny towers,
They laugh and play for hours and hours.

A rabbit hops on tiny feet,
With wiggly nose, he's quite the treat.
He chats with birds about the sun,
And asks them, 'Is this day for fun?'

Trees wear hats made out of leaves,
Like little kids who dare to tease.
The wind sings songs, a cheeky tune,
While critters dance beneath the moon.

So join this jolly woodland crew,
Where laughter grows as wild as dew.
In every nook, a jest is spun,
In whispered joy, the day is won.

Symphony in the Saplings

In the glen, where giggles play,
Tiny creatures shout hooray!
With woodland friends, they form a band,
Strumming tunes on soft, green land.

Frogs croak jokes with silly croons,
While raccoons tap on shiny spoons.
The melody of rustling leaves,
Is music made that never leaves.

A fox, a cheeky little sprite,
Dances under stars so bright.
With twirls and spins, he prances by,
His laughter echoing the sky.

Though nature's tunes can shift and sway,
So many games to make the day.
Beneath the trees, all colors blend,
A playful song without an end.

The Dance of the Leaves

Leaves jiggle, wiggle, in the breeze,
Doing twirls with joyful ease.
A shuffle here, a spin and hop,
Giving every branch a top-notch pop.

Acorns roll like bowling balls,
As chipmunks cheer in leafy halls.
Swaying branches join the fun,
"Let's see who can outdance the sun!"

A breeze tickles a sleepy stump,
"Wake up, buddy! Give a jump!"
The forest floor erupts in cheer,
As surprises spring from far and near.

So waltz along the forest lane,
With every creature, fun is gain.
In every rustle, beat, and leap,
There's joy to share, a charm to keep.

Echoes Beneath the Canopy

Beneath the trees, where shadows play,
A band of pals will laugh all day.
The echoes bounce from trunk to trunk,
As laughter blooms like playful funk.

A chipmunk races up a pine,
Squeaks out jokes designed to shine.
With every step, a funny prank,
Rows of bushes, his little tank.

The owls keep watch, wide-eyed and wise,
As secrets float beneath the skies.
They giggle hoots and wink with glee,
For woodland shenanigans, oh, let's see!

In dappled light, they all unite,
Creating joy from day to night.
With every chuckle, leaf, and cheer,
The forest whispers, "Bring friends near!"

Assembling in the Arboreal Sanctuary

In the woods, the squirrels chatter,
Gathering nuts like they matter.
Birds tweet jokes in the tree above,
Filling the air with laughter and love.

Mice join in with a dance so spry,
Waltzing under the watchful sky.
A rabbit hops, with a grin so wide,
As he twirls and leaps with pride.

Fungi giggle in the dampened shade,
While shadows of whimsy start to parade.
The breeze carries secrets of fun and light,
In this refuge where all feels just right.

Nature's jesters in unison play,
In this sanctuary, they frolic all day.
Each critter brings humor, never a care,
In the arboreal realm, joy fills the air.

The Harmony of Sunlit Spaces

In sunlit spots where the grass does sway,
Lizards sunbathe, laughing away.
The bees buzz jokes as they gather their gold,
Telling stories of harvest, amusingly bold.

A frog croaks out a terrible pun,
His friends all croak back, oh what fun!
Butterflies flutter in colorful suits,
Spreading their wings like musical flutes.

The breeze, a playful tickle on skin,
Gathers all creatures, the small and the thin.
Chirps and caws make a raucous delight,
As day melts to dusk, and brings forth the night.

Even the flowers seem to grin wide,
With petals that dance in a joyful tide.
In these bright spaces, laughter is king,
As each creature joins in for the joy they bring.

Nurtured by Nature's Whisper

The leaves rustle softly, a giggling sound,
Gossiping squirrels hop all around.
Rabbits convene for a thumping good laugh,
In the quiet glen, they take their own path.

A wise old owl shares witticisms rare,
While chipmunks munch on snacks without care.
The brook bubbles up with a ticklish spree,
Each splash a chuckle, wild and free.

The sun, like a jester, sparkles so bright,
Casting shadows that dance in pure light.
In this sanctuary, whimsy unfolds,
With tales of the forest being eagerly told.

Nature's embrace is a giggly delight,
Where each creature thrives, morning till night.
With a chuckle and cheer, they all play their part,
In this world where laughter fills the heart.

Collective Chorus of the Green

In the glade, a chorus begins to sing,
With crickets and frogs lending their bling.
An orchestra of rustles plays along,
Creating a melody, silly and strong.

The flowers sway in whimsical glee,
As butterflies waltz with raucous decree.
The trees, tall and proud, nod with a sway,
Joining the fun in a most charming way.

Mice interpret the music with flair,
Dancing on leaves without a single care.
Together they giggle in a leafy parade,
As the forest echoes the joy they've made.

With each chorus, the afternoon fades,
Yet laughter and cheer never evade.
In this vibrant patch, they weave and they twine,
In the green embrace, all souls intertwine.

Whirling Whispers of the Wild

In the woods where squirrels dance,
A rabbit twirls, seizing the chance.
He spins and hops with quite a flair,
While birds just giggle from a branch up there.

Chipmunks chatter, making a scene,
While grasshoppers boast of legs so lean.
But one big toad croaks out a tune,
As he juggles bugs beneath the moon.

Frogs in hats parade along,
They ribbit out their froggy song.
With each leap, they launch a cheer,
Making all the critters near disappear!

So join this madcap, merry band,
In this leafy, lively land.
Where every chuckle, wink, and tease,
Sings of fun amidst the trees.

Tides of the Tree Tops

Up above, the branches sway,
Where a squirrel plots his acorn play.
A jay tweets jokes in silly rhyme,
As the sun sets down, oh what a time!

The wind brings whispers, tickles and sways,
While owls hoot in their wise old ways.
A raccoon rolls, all covered in grime,
Stating he's the king of bedtime prime!

The leaves do dance, they shimmy and glide,
While squirrels cheer from their leafy ride.
Every rustle quickens the strife,
In this quirky, treetop life.

At dusk, rest beckons on every bough,
With laughter echoing, take a bow.
For up in the canopy high and bright,
The shenanigans carry on through the night.

A Ballet of Bark and Breeze

In the glade, a waltz unfolds,
With dancing leaves in greens and golds.
The branches wave like arms in flight,
While critters join with pure delight.

A porcupine dons a tutu bold,
With prickly grace, he's never cold.
A fox flips high, with style so sweet,
While turtles groan, keeping up the beat.

In this grand ballet of bark and breeze,
Even the ants move with such ease.
They twirl and spin with utmost flair,
With tiny pirouettes in the air.

When night falls soft, there's no one to cease,
This whimsical dancing, full of peace.
Every critter knows it takes some art,
To share a laugh right from the heart.

The Soulful Soundscape of Sap

The tree trunk hums a sticky tune,
As sap drips down, it gleams like June.
A woodpecker joins, tapping away,
Creating beats for the critters' play.

Beneath the bark, the rhythm runs,
While bees buzz out their busy puns.
The ants form lines, a marching band,
With sugar crumbs all perfectly planned.

A bear strolls in, with dancing paws,
And every flick adds to the applause.
The frogs leap high, croaking out laughter,
In this soulful spectacle, happily after.

So when you wander where the sap flows,
Listen closely to the joy it shows.
For in this forest, full of zest,
Nature's antics are the very best!

www.ingramcontent.com/pod-product-compliance
Lightning Source LLC
Chambersburg PA
CBHW051648160426
43209CB00004B/844

*9 7 8 1 8 0 5 6 7 3 4 6 0 *